HISTORY OF THE DALMATIAN

The history of the dog known as the Dalmatian, or "Dal" for short, is wonderfully vague and delightfully ambiguous. Its beginnings and origins are shrouded in the cloudy mists of time. If we allow ourselves a little romantic leeway, we may be able to trace him back to the dawn of our great civilizations. We do know that the Dalmatian is a very old breed, unlike many newcomers that are "man made." There are ancient Egyptian bas-reliefs 50 centuries old showing spotted dogs similar in appearance to the modern Dalmatian. Later Egyptian artifacts found in tombs show dogs resembling Dalmatians in sedentary postures, suggesting their use as guard dogs. Ancient Greek wall frescos and friezes depict Dalmatian-like dogs in hunting scenes. There is a model of a white dog with round black spots found in an excavation dating from the Mycenaean period of ancient Greece, about 1600 B.C., that conforms somewhat loosely to the modern standard of the breed.

The black and white spotted Dalmatian has a wonderfully ambiguous history.

Curiously, despite its name, there is little or no evidence of any historical link between Dalmatians and Dalmatia, the western coastal province of Croatia, a 5,000 square mile mountainous region abreast of the Adriatic, due east of northern Italy. This area was part of Illyria, a land subject to and tributory to ancient Rome and the scene of many Roman battles. Legend has it that Dalmatian-like spotted dogs accompanied Roman legions on their marches and campaigns. This included the great civil war between Julius Caesar and Pompey, which took place mostly in Illyria. This was long before the dog was called "Dalmatian," of course, and can hardly account for the name. Interestingly though, accounts of ___ coast ___ Dubrovnik ___ a ___ ing the dogs found there.

There was a treatise written in

England in 1570 by a Dutch physician to King Edward III describing a new variety of spotted white dog recently imported from France called the "Gallician" or French dog. The dog described was probably very similar to the modern Dalmatian and likely marks the beginning of its modern recorded development in Great Britain. There are references to this French dog in the late 16th and early 17th centuries. Undoubtedly these are the same white spotted dogs used as symbols to mock and depict the Catholic Church in the anti-clerical tracts of the Cromwell dictatorship between 1653 and 1658. The white and black spotted dogs were symbolic of the Roman church and religious rule from Rome.

Did the Dalmatian originate in India? This 18th century depiction of a dog known as the Rengal Harrier shows much of the Dalmatian type.

While the dog imported from France may well be the first authentic recorded ancestor of today's Dalmatian, the dog certainly did not just materialize when it got to England. We do know that the breed was a great favorite and constant companion of gypsies who spread the breed throughout Europe. It may well be that the breed was brought out of India in ancient times during the early migrations of gypsies from India to Europe in the fifth and sixth centuries.

One theory paralleling this romantic story holds that the Dalmatian was originally a distinctive breed of pointer that was popular with gypsies who introduced it into the Balkans in their early migrations. It moved around from place to place with these migrating people through the ages. During the late middle ages, large bands of migrating gypsies settled temporarily in Dalmatia, then an Austrian province, and while they and their dogs eventually moved on, the name "Dalmatian" stuck to the dog and remained forever associated with it.

However the Dalmatian came to be and whatever role the gypsies played, it is known that for hundreds of years before the breed's importation into Britain white pointer dogs with spots that resembled the Dalmatian were found throughout central Europe in the area between northern India and the west of Europe. They were especially popular in the Balkans and in the other mountainous regions of central Europe, where they were widely used as hunting or game dogs. It is now commonly accepted that the Dalmatian or something nearly identical to it has existed throughout Europe for well over 450 years, and probably even a lot longer.

There is a reverse migration theory supported by some evidence that the breed originated in northern Denmark. Indeed, in some countries and languages the breed is called a small Dane. This theory holds that the Dalmatian is descended from the Mastiff and is a close relation or smaller version of the Harlequin Great Dane. There are, and always have been, many Dalmatians in Denmark. Supposedly these dogs were taken south to warmer climates, producing the so-called "Turkish" dog, another name for the Dalmatian-like dog that flourished during the period of Turkish rule in the Balkans when Dalmatia was a province of European Turkey.

There is a thin connection that suggests both Italian and Spanish origins for the Dalmatian. The Spanish theory reasons that the Pointer, the dog most closely resembling the Dalmatian and likely a close relative, has a Spanish origin. The Italian connection is derived from the dog's place in a few Renaissance paintings and the fact that Dalmatians were used as a papal symbol. This suggests that to Cromwell and his severe fanatical Roundhead party of Parliamentarians the dog had either an Italian origin or a connection that, taken with its white and black coloring, made it a splendid mocking symbol of the Roman church.

Miss Griselda Hervey and her two Dalmatian friends. The Dalmatian has become a very popular breed, and deservedly so.

Whatever its origins, the breed flourished in England, where it has been known as the Dalmatian for over two hundred years. The first written use of the term Dalmatian doesn't appear until 1780. The breed, whatever it was called before then, developed and flourished before that for over two hundred years under other names. The "Gallician" or French dog was probably the first name used. Other names included "The Harrier of Bengal," giving credence to its Indian origin; the Danish dog; the Turkish dog; and even the "Plum Pudding" dog. However, the most common and most enduring name over time has been "Coach" or "Carriage" dog.

While the breed and its progenitors were used as pointers and working hunters, the Dalmatian was soon put to other uses in Britain. The Dalmatian's first importation and use was by the gentry and nobility for hunting. Over time, the Dalmatian has become synonymous with the horse-drawn coach, the carriage, and the famous coach and four, a carriage drawn by four horses commonly used as a form of passage over long distances in Britain.

Traditionally, the Dalmatian has been not only a loving family member but a watchful guard dog.

As the breed developed and was cultivated in England, the dog was traditionally trained and conditioned to run with horse-drawn vehicles. The Dalmatian is the only breed specifically bred for this purpose. For this reason, the Dalmatian has been and probably always will be associated with the horse-drawn vehicle and thought of as a companion animal to both horse and man. During the late 17th, 18th, and 19th centuries, when man traveled by coach, the Dalmatian was frequently found running alongside, often under one of the coach axles or mixed between the horses. It was a scene commonplace in England, and to a lesser extent in France. Apparently, the preferred position for the dog among coachmen was under the front axle, hard by the horses' rear heels. The term "coaching" described the act of a dog running under the axle of the coach.

The Dalmatian was more than an attractive accessory to the coach. It served the important practical function of guarding the coach and its contents at every stop, scheduled and unscheduled.

This is an official US Army photograph of the Dalmatian war dogs of Capt. John S. Durigg, 89th Div. Veterinarian, Camp Carson, Colorado.

Thieves were discouraged from approaching the carriage from any direction, and they soon realized that simply distracting the driver and other riders availed them little or naught if the carriage was protected by a Dal or two.

With the decline and eventual disappearance of coach travel, one of the Dalmatian's "jobs" disappeared as well. However, the British love for the Dalmatian did not diminish. It was still used as a gun dog, guard dog, for badger and small game baiting, and as an attention-getting dog for the beau monde. It was likely that it was the breed's striking appearance that made the British so fond of Dalmatians. As early as 1803, the Dalmatian is listed in a publication identifying 23 known breeds of dog in Britain. In 1860, at one of the first dog shows ever held in Britain, the Dalmatian was one of the competing classes for conformation judging. A year later at another show, the breed was one of only five breeds shown. It is fair to say, that whatever the ancient origin of the Dalmatian, the modern Dal really owes its development to Great Britain where its good looks made it a great favorite.

Those devoted to the breed continued to refine the dog to produce a beautiful specimen. British exports were used to improve the breed in both Europe and America. It was the British type that became the standard and measure for control worldwide. The breed standard, hammered out in successive generations in the 19th century, described a companion dog with a wonderful disposition, great intelligence, and beauty. All of this combined with its remarkable endurance and compact sturdy physique made the dog the darling of the sporting crowd. The Dal was used in circuses and side shows as a performing "trick dog" and in music hall acts. The Dal became a symbol of outdoor sporting life, a reputation retained to this day. Always highly photogenic, the Dal appears in many paintings depicting country life in Britain, and later in America, all through the 19th century. Ironically, it appears that any Dalmatians found in Dalmatia were the offspring of English imports. There is no native strain of Dalmatians in Dalmatia.

The British foundation stock and the resulting standards that evolved were responsible in part for the geographical dispersion and modest popularity of the breed worldwide in the 19th century.

The Dalmatian Club of Great Britain was started in 1890. The club adopted a standard of conformation that modified several earlier standards. Regional Dalmatian clubs adopted this standard in successive years.

There was a decline in the breed's popularity, as with most breeds in Britain, during World War I. The terrible war years and the end of the coach era seemed to thin the ranks well into the early 1920s. A southern Dalmatian Club was formed in England in 1920 to buck the trend. This club evolved into the British Dalmatian Club. There was a similar decline in breeding and club activities during World War II, when dog shows on anything more than a very small local scale would have been inappropriate. Immediately after the war, there was a flurry of activity. The Dalmatian seemed to retain its popularity, at least on a scale comparable to the period between the wars, all through the decade of post-war austerity in Britain.

Ownership was pretty much limited to such Dalmatian partisans as longtime breeders and the traditional crowd of well-connected Dal people. It was the book *101 Dalmatians* by Dodie Smith, which appeared in 1956, and the later Disney film of the same name, that focused world-wide attention on the breed and cast it well outside the limited circle of aficionados that had loved and cultivated it. The result was the usual impact of large scale, and sometime indiscriminate, breeding of the Dalmatian. This corresponded naturally with the large-scale growth of the British Dalmatian Club as the dog's popularity rapidly accelerated.

With the Dal's new-found popularity came overproduction and the need for rescue work by the club for the first time in the history of the breed. As with every breed that experiences sudden popularity, vast, rapid overbreeding, caused by breeding for profit, threatened to compromise the time-honored breed standard. The British Dalmatian Club worked tirelessly to maintain the traditional, healthy standard for the breed. The British standard thus developed, fostered, and maintained by the British Dalmatian Club has remained the basic standard used worldwide and has resulted in an essential global uniformity of the breed. While modifications have been made in the U.S. standard, from time to time in the past few decades, the British standard can truly be said to be the foundation standard upon which the others are built.

Because of their natural abilities with large animals, their easy-to-see coats, and their endurance and intelligence, Dalmatians became the perfect choice for firehouse dogs after the development of the horse-drawn engine of the city fire departments.

THE DALMATIAN IN THE UNITED STATES

Dalmatians were imported into the United States by the latter half of the 18th century, making the perilous transatlantic voyage necessary in that age. It is known from his correspondence that George Washington himself bought a Dalmatian, which he called "a coach dog," to breed to another. The early history of the Dalmatian in the U.S. loosely parallels that of Britain, as the dog was used for hunting and coach work. It was an early companion and decorative accessory for the gentry and the carriage trade. In the 19th century, with western expansion and the vast distances thereby created, carriage transportation gave way first to the stage coach and then to canal and railroad transportation, all inappropriate for coach dogs. The Dalmatian didn't vanish, but remained a hunter and coach dog in the older areas of the North and Southeast. It was found on the plantations of the ante-bellum South and continued to function in its traditional ornamental role for the leisure classes of both the North and South. It was the growth of cities after the industrial revolution, but especially after the Civil War, that created a new and exciting career for the Dalmatian, and one which swelled their numbers. This was the development of the urban city fire department with its horse-drawn engines. It was this unique use of the horse-drawn carriage that gave the Dalmatian the chance to become the breed forever associated with fire companies and their engines. To many, the Dalmatian is and always will be "the firehouse dog." The Dal's traditional instinctive compatibility with horses, its easy to see white black- or liver-spotted coat, its endurance, and its intelligence gave it the advantage over every other possible competing mascot for the firemen. There was hardly a fire company in New York, Boston, Chicago, and other great cities that didn't have a Dal mascot. These firehouse dogs weren't just pets—they served very useful functions while clearing the way for the horse-drawn apparatus.

Due to their natural affinity for horses and ratting ability, Dalmatians are often used as farm dogs.

After the turn of the century, as the motor car and the truck replaced horse-drawn vehicles, the Dal's role was reduced once again to riding the engine with the firemen or staying at the firehouse as a watchdog until the engines returned. So universal and popular was the "Firehouse Dog" that the Westminster Kennel Club offered a separate competition class for Dalmatians owned by New York City firemen at one of its shows. The Dalmatian as a symbol of firefighting and firefighters has persisted to this day. It is still used as the symbol for Fire Prevention Week. Today, there are firehouses across the U.S. that keep Dalmatians as pets, serving as a reminder of times past and the glorious firefighting tradition.

The Dalmatian Club of America (DCA) was founded in 1905. Membership was limited to 50 members. Many of the leading contemporary kennels and breeding programs of today's show quality Dals derive their descent from the breeding stock and kennels of these charter members and others who joined the DCA early on.

As in Britain, there was a severe decline in club and dog show activity during World War II, with a substantial revival right after the war. While DCA membership was expanded to more than 50 members in 1937, membership remained modest with less than two hundred members into the late 1960s. It was in the 1970s that the membership, which had been mostly seaboard, expanded both in size and geographical location. The DCA now has well over 1200 members nationwide. There are numerous local regional clubs scattered across the country that mirror the Dalmatian's national popularity.

The Westminster Kennel Club offered a separate competition class for Dalmatians owned by New York City firemen at one of its shows. The breed's firehouse dog reputation is likely never to die.

DALMATIAN CHARACTERISTICS

The Dalmatian is a very versatile and adaptable dog. A brief review of its history will highlight its many-sided nature. The Dal was a coach dog, hunter, ratter, guardian and firehouse dog. It has been a mascot, house pet, ornament, and above all else, a companion, first to British high society, and then to the rest of the world. The Dal is by nature a gentle dog, very obedient, if trained properly, and comparatively easy to train. Since it can be trained for such a variety of purposes, such as defense, guard work, and guide dog work, it can be said that the Dal is truly an all-around dog.

Prospective buyers should bear in mind, however, that the Dal is essentially a scenting hound by nature and an outdoor physical creature. Most Dal owners report that rigorous physical exercise has a calming and tranquilizing effect on their Dals, who are usually very rambunctious in their first three years. The Dal is ideally suited for people who lead an active outdoor lifestyle. It is easier to train and control your Dal if the dog is given brisk, frequent workouts.

Nevertheless, there are many happy Dal owners who live a sedentary existence in apartments in urban settings with this most adaptable dog. While this may be a satisfactory arrangement, it doesn't always work out. Depending on breeding and bloodlines, Dals can be restless and hyperactive, especially until about three or four years of age. The ideal arrangement is a fenced yard where the dog can run freely and exercise off the lead. Some breeders find their younger dogs go stir-crazy if kept in a confined space for too long. This is especially true for the youngsters in the 9-18 month age bracket. There are breeders who will not sell their puppies to families with children under three or four years of age, especially if the children appear timid. There is, of course, great variation among individual dogs, even in the same litter. Temperaments can vary and

In the first three years of life, Dalmatians are rambunctious and curious creatures.

run from one end of the spectrum to the other. Remember that for centuries the Dal was bred to run or coach 30 to 40 miles per day. While they have been house pets for many generations, there is always the possibility that you are bringing a pent-up bundle of nervous energy into your home. An owner who cannot provide the needed exercise will find it even more necessary to properly train his Dal by establishing a strong position of leadership and fostering a healthy master-dog relationship with the pet. There is an old maxim among Dal owners that holds, "Lead or be led." The Dal owner should always be in control and expect this most obedient dog to obey if given proper, effective leadership.

The Dal is normally very good with children, and will usually tolerate a fair amount of abuse from a child. Its superior intelligence helps it sense the child's immaturity so that it makes some allowances for the child's behavior. The Dal will usually avoid getting "cornered" by a child and will usually find some harmless way around trouble. Of course, there are limits, and even the most tolerant Dal can be pushed too far. Again, good training, combined with the Dal's even temperament and intelligence, should overcome any potential problem.

Like most medium-sized dogs, Dalmatians have lots of energy and need plenty of space to run around.

The Dal is not a small dog. It is a muscular 45-60 pounds of stored energy. Dals are sometimes reluctant to lie down until all of the family members are settled and in sedate relaxed postures. They are not at all lazy and seem to have a sincere humility, giving them a remarkable personality. They are not by nature frequent barkers and seldom engage in idle

Dalmatians have unique personalities. They can even smile. Originally, many Dalmatians were thought to be somewhat aloof, as well as high strung, and less affectionate than some other breeds. Forced conversion to pet life was a big departure from its former firehouse and coach duties. Years of household domesticity and active breeding have made a

Dals are very people oriented, and do well with children. These young ladies are learning the miracle of life from their Dalmatian friends.

barking sessions, rarely joining in a cacophony of howls with other neighborhood dogs. Their barking tends to be more selective and meaningful, so that the owner can usually attach some significance to it. As one would expect, this trait made the Dal very popular as a guard and watch dog.

big improvement, so much so that today many Dals are as warmly affectionate as any other lovable breed.

Dals are usually good with other pets such as cats and birds, depending on their training and the degree of order in the household. There can, however, be problems with other large dogs of

Dalmatians have unique personalities and can even be seen smiling at times. These three Dalmatians each show a different expression to the camera.

Dalmatians should always sleep inside. A crate lined with soft warm blankets is ideal bedding for a Dal puppy.

the same sex as dominance feuds and pecking order struggles tend to develop. People with two or more Dals of the same sex need to be aware of this and should be vigilant in watching for problems.

Dals are, by dog standards, neat. They are extremely sensitive at times and seem to crave human company. Dals that are ignored or denied companionship sometimes become very melancholy or depressed. Their feelings seem to be easily hurt, but they are one of the breeds that can actually smile. When happy, praised or excited in a good way, the corners of their mouths actually turn up, showing some teeth that could scare the initiated. They have remarkable memories and never forget or forgive a rival dog who does them wrong. They are reliable

companions who love to play and play well with children. As stated above, they can take a lot of abuse but sometimes can accidentally injure a child during rough play by knocking the child down or hitting the child with their tail. The Dal is a powerful dog for its size. Its wagging tail can feel like the lash of a rawhide whip to a small, toddling child. It is a lively dog, and depending on its breeding and bloodline, may well be too active for some households with very small children. This is why some breeders are reluctant to sell Dal puppies to families with toddlers, especially if the people know little or nothing of dog ownership fundamentals and there is potential for wildness in the untrained pup.

The Dal should always sleep indoors as it has for centuries in coach houses and firehouses. The Dal is great with large four-legged animals, especially horses. The Dal is a natural watchdog, protective by nature of its family and home. It is spectacular in appearance and while classified as a Non-Sporting breed by the AKC, the Dalmatian is very much an athlete.

Dals are very adaptable. There are many Dalmatian owners who live in apartments and cannot exercise their Dals the way they should, but the animals and owners are happy together nonetheless. Of course, city Dals that are not exercised as often or as much as they should be are likely to lack the musculature and sound development evident in a dog raised in a country setting. In plain terms, they will be out of shape and will be somewhat softer than they should be with poor muscle tone, just like many people with the same lifestyle. There are lots of Dals that have become "couch potatoes" like their masters, a rather unfortunate adaptation.

The Dal is a great favorite of celebrities the world over, including Dick Clark, singer Gloria Estafan, who owns two Dals, and actress Michelle Lee who rescued and owned a deaf Dal.

The Dalmatian is a wonderful dog, which if properly trained and understood makes a splendid addition to many households. It will return your love and affection many fold and give you years of devoted loyalty.

Through many years of being coach dogs, Dalmatians have gained a special "way" with large four-legged animals, especially horses — but cattle also qualify.

STANDARD FOR THE DALMATIAN

The old British standard of 1890 that had been developed for a century in Britain was essentially the standard employed in the U.S. until 1950. There had been some minor modifications suggested in 1905 by the newly formed DCA. The AKC standard of 1913 specified size as between 19 characteristic, greater emphasis was accordingly placed on movement so that form might more closely conform to function. This was done partially to blunt the concern that emphasis on conformational physical traits might, with increasing popularity and breeding activity, spoil the

Sleek and powerful for his size, the Dalmatian is bred for soundness because he performs so many functions.

and 23 inches at the withers, with no weight difference between dogs and bitches. In 1950, the AKC changed the standard to place more emphasis on gait. Taking into account the dog's origins and natural propensities, the American standard recognized the need to emphasize soundness. In an effort to reward this breed by taking it too far from its original purpose. Exaggerating traits of form, rather than of substance, has ruined many breeds. This was the pitfall they were trying to avoid.

While height was again specified by the standard, dogs outside the standard were not disqualified in the show ring. This

The Dalmatian is alert and intelligent, which is evident in his expression and ability to learn quickly.

changed in 1962 when the American standard was again revised by the AKC at the request of the DCA, disqualifying dogs above the height standard. The language of the standard preamble dealing with the dog's general appearance was made more specific regarding alertness, temperament, and intelligence. Specific disqualifications were enumerated. These included any color spot except black or liver; any size over 24 inches at the withers; a bite either under- or overshot; large patches of dark hair and blotches rather than clearly defined spots; and finally what are termed "tri-colors" on dogs with both liver and black spots on a white coat.

This is ironic and shows how far the standard has evolved, since the first Dalmatian ever registered in the AKC stud book was a tri-color white, black, and brown dog.

The standard was modified again in 1989 to produce the current standard. The general appearance section of the standard perhaps best describes the breed:

"The Dalmatian is a distinctively spotted dog; poised and alert; strong, muscular and active; free of shyness; intelligent in expression; symmetrical in outline; and without exaggeration or coarseness. The Dalmatian is capable of great endurance, combined with a fair amount of speed."

As stated, at present the DCA has over 1200 members. By and large, the membership seems

As is inherent in the breed, this Dalmatian puppy stands poised and alert ready to pounce on anything that moves.

A Dalmatian and a Pointer. Dalmatians are medium-sized dogs, standing between 19 and 23 inches.

content with the 1989 standard and there is little agitation among the membership to change the standard. This doesn't mean that there is complete consensus on every subject or aspect of the standard or other breed matters. As with any large organization, there are disagreements and factions with opposing views. While the standard calls for dogs to be between 19-23 inches high at the withers, an extra inch is allowed before disqualification. The old British standard never did, and still does not, penalize dogs larger than 24 inches in height. As with some other breeds, notably the Jack Russell Terrier, many American exhibitors have claimed that the British judges tend to favor larger dogs. There is no disqualification for dogs smaller than 19 inches at present.

There is no specification in the standard for weight, but bitches should run between 45-55 pounds, while dogs ideally run from 50- 65 pounds. Weight is never cause for disqualification. The tail should not curl, but should be erect with a slight turn-up at the tip. The ears should be

Although there are some exceptions, the Dalmatian's eyes should be dark, ears spotted and nose solid in color.

spotted, but solid white ears are within the standard. Eyes should be dark. Dalmatian puppies are born white, with spots appearing at about ten days of age.

The DCA, as with the British club, is vitally interested in maintaining a healthy standard for the breed and is involved in active support of projects and studies devoted to Dalmatian health problems and special needs.

AMERICAN KENNEL CLUB STANDARD FOR THE DALMATIAN

General Appearance—The Dalmatian is a distinctively spotted dog; poised and alert; strong, muscular and active; free of shyness; intelligent in expression; symmetrical in outline; and without exaggeration or coarseness. The Dalmatian is capable of great endurance, combined with fair amount of speed. Deviations from the described ideal should be penalized in direct proportion to the degree of the deviation.

Size, Proportion, Substance—Desirable height at the withers is between 19 and 23 inches. Undersize or oversize is a fault. Any dog or bitch over 24 inches at the withers is disqualified. The overall length of the body from the forechest to the buttocks is approximately equal to the height at the withers. The Dalmatian has good substance and is strong and sturdy in bone, but never coarse.

Head—The head is in balance with the overall dog. It is of fair length and is free of loose skin. The Dalmatian's *expression* is alert and intelligent, indicating a stable and out-going

The Dalmatian's tail should be erect with a slight upward curve at the end. It should not curl up over the back.

Sleek and glossy, the coat of the Dalmatian is short, dense, fine, and close fitting. It shouldn't be woolly or silky.

temperament. The **eyes** are set moderately well apart, are medium sized and somewhat rounded in appearance, and are set well into the skull. Eye color is brown or blue, or any combination thereof; the darker the better and usually darker in black-spotted than in liver-spotted dogs. Abnormal position of the eyelids or eyelashes (ectropion, entropion, trichiasis) is a major fault. Incomplete pigmentation of the eye rims is a major fault. The **ears** are of moderate size, proportionately wide at the base and gradually tapering to a rounded tip. They are set rather high, and are carried close to the head, and are thin and fine in texture. When the Dalmatian is alert, the top of the ear is level with the top of the skull and the tip of the ear reaches to the bottom line of the cheek. The top of the skull is flat with a slight vertical furrow and is approximately as wide as it is long. The *stop* is moderately well defined. The cheeks blend smoothly into the powerful **muzzle**, the top of which is level

Some Dalmatians have incomplete nose pigmentation, referred to as a "butterfly nose." This is a major fault, but it does not affect the Dalmatian's ability to compete or be a loving pet.

and parallel to the top of the skull. The muzzle and the top of the skull are about equal in length. The **nose** is completely pigmented on the leather, black in black-spotted dogs and brown in liver-spotted dogs. Incomplete nose pigmentation is a major fault. The **lips** are clean and close fitting. The teeth meet in a **scissors bite**. Overshot or undershot bites are disqualifications.

Neck, Topline, Body—The **neck** is nicely arched, fairly long, free from throatiness, and blends smoothly into the shoulders. The **topline** is smooth. The **chest** *i*s deep, capacious and of moderate width, having good spring of rib without being barrel shaped. The brisket reaches to the elbow. The underline of the rib cage curves gradually into a moderate tuck-up. The **back** is level and strong. The **loin** is short, muscular and slightly arched. The flanks narrow through the loin. The **croup** is nearly level with the back. The **tail** is a natural extension of the topline. It is not inserted too low down, It is strong at the insertion and tapers to the tip, which reaches the hock. It is never docked. The tail is carried with a slight upward curve but should never curl over the back. Ring tails and low-set tails are faults.

Forequarters—The **shoulders** are smoothly muscled and well laid back. The **upper arm** is approximately equal in length to the shoulder blade and joins it at an angle sufficient to insure that the foot falls under the shoulder. The **elbows** are close to the body. The **legs** are straight, strong and sturdy in bone. There is a slight angle at the **pastern** denoting flexibility.

Hindquarters—The **hindquarters** are powerful, having smooth, yet well defined

Cow hocks (hocks turned inward) and barrel hocks (hocks bowed outward) are major faults. Hind legs should be parallel to each other from the hocks to the pads of the feet.

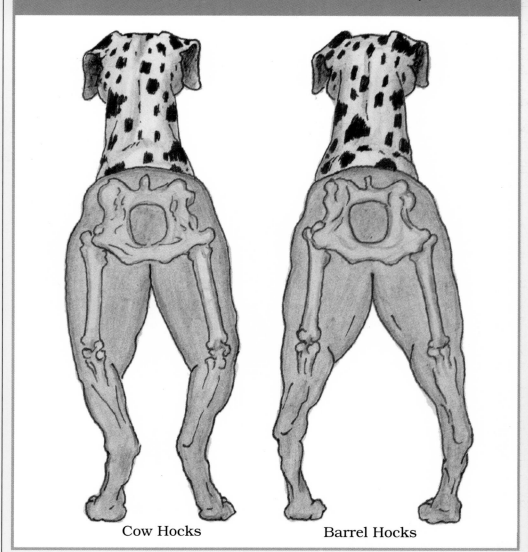

Cow Hocks   Barrel Hocks

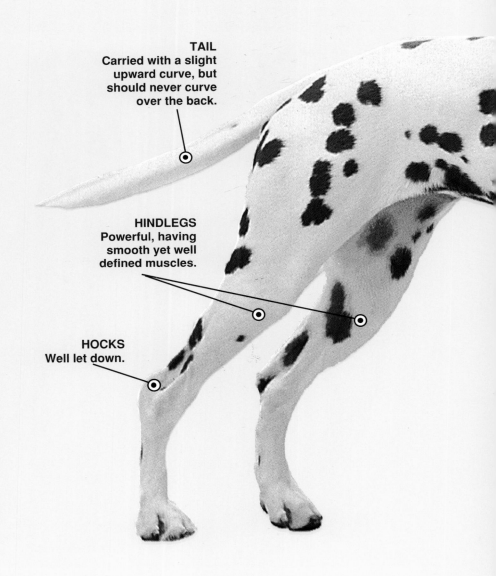

TAIL
Carried with a slight
upward curve, but
should never curve
over the back.

HINDLEGS
Powerful, having
smooth yet well
defined muscles.

HOCKS
Well let down.

EARS
Wide at the base
and gradually tapering
to a round tip.

EYES
Medium sized, round,
and set well into skull.

NECK
Nicely arched
and fairly long.

MUZZLE
Powerful and equal in
length to the top of the
skull.

TOPLINE
Smooth

LIPS
Clean and close
fitting.

CHEST
Deep and capacious.

FORELEGS
Straight strong
and sturdy in
bone.

FEET
Round and compact
with thick elastic pads
and well arched toes.

PASTERNS
Slightly
angled,
denoting
flexibility.

muscles. The ***stifle*** is well bent. The ***hocks*** are well let down. When the Dalmatian is standing, the hind legs, viewed from the rear, are parallel to each other from the point of the hock to the heel of the pad. Cow hocks are a major fault.

Feet—***Feet*** are very important. Both front and rear feet are round and compact with thick, elastic pads and well arched toes. Flat feet are a major fault. Toenails are black and/or white in black-spotted dogs and brown and/or white in liver-spotted dogs. Dew claws may be removed.

Coat—The coat is short, dense, fine and close fitting. It is neither woolly nor silky. It is sleek, glossy and healthy in appearance.

Color and Markings—***Color and markings*** and their overall appearance are very important points to be evaluated. The ground color is pure white. In black-spotted dogs the spots are dense black. In liver-spotted dogs the spots are liver brown. Any color markings other than black or liver are disqualified. ***Spots*** are round a well-defined, the more distinct the better. They vary from the size of a dime to the size of a half-dollar. They are pleasingly and evenly distributed. The less the spots intermingle the better. Spots are usually smaller on the head, legs and tail than on the body. Ears are preferably spotted.

As beautiful as any dog, the Dalmatian is a unique, intelligent, and outgoing dog.

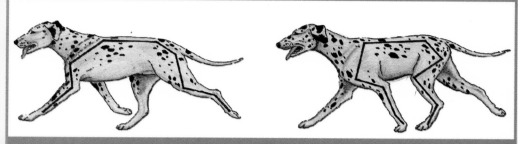

With topline level, the Dalmatian's gait has extended reach in the front and powerful drive from the rear. He moves with a smooth and effortless motion.

Tri-color (which occurs rarely in this breed) is a disqualification. It consists of tan markings found on the head, neck, chest, leg or tail of a black- or liver-spotted dog. Bronzing of black spots, and fading and/or darkening of liver spots due to environmental conditions or normal processes of coat change are not tri-coloration. ***Patches*** are a disqualification. A patch is a solid mass of black or liver hair containing no white hair. It is appreciably larger than a normal sized spot. Patches are a dense, brilliant color with sharply defined, smooth edges. Patches are present at birth. Large color masses formed by intermingled or overlapping spots are not patches. Such masses should indicate individual spots by uneven edges and/or white hairs scattered throughout the mass.

Gait—In keeping with the Dalmatian's historical use as a coach dog, gait and endurance are of great importance. Movement is steady and effortless. Balanced angulation fore and aft combined with powerful muscles and good condition produce smooth, efficient action. There is a powerful drive from the rear coordinated with extended reach in the front. The topline remains level. Elbows, hocks and feet turn neither in nor out. As the speed of the trot increases, there is a tendency to single track.

Temperament—Temperament is stable and outgoing, yet dignified. Shyness is a major fault.

DISQUALIFICATIONS

Any dog or bitch over 24 inches at the withers. Overshot or undershot bite. Any color markings other than blacks or liver. Patches.

SCALE OF POINTS	
General Appearance	5
Size, Proportion, Substance	10
Head	10
Neck, Topline, Body	10
Forequarters	5
Hindquarters	5
Feet	5
Coat	5
Color and Markings	25
Gait	10
Temperament	10
Total	100

YOUR NEW DALMATIAN PUPPY

SELECTION

When you do pick out a Dalmatian puppy as a pet, don't be hasty; the longer you study puppies, the better you will understand them. Make it your transcendent concern to select only one that radiates good health and spirit and is lively on his feet, whose eyes are bright, whose coat shines, and who comes forward eagerly to make and to cultivate your acquaintance. Don't fall for any shy little darling that wants to retreat to his bed or his box, or plays coy behind other puppies or people, or hides his head under your arm or jacket appealing to your protective instinct. *Pick the Dalmatian puppy who forthrightly picks you! The feeling of attraction should be mutual!*

Puppy selection should not be done hastily. Be sure to take time to observe the puppy you want with his littermates.

DOCUMENTS

Now, a little paper work is in order. When you purchase a purebred Dalmatian puppy, you should receive a transfer of ownership, registration material, and other "papers" (a list of the immunization shots, if any, the puppy may have been given; a note on whether or not the puppy has been wormed; a diet and feeding schedule to which the puppy is accustomed) and you are welcomed as a fellow owner to a long, pleasant association with a most lovable pet, and more (news)paper work.

GENERAL PREPARATION

You have chosen to own a particular Dalmatian puppy. You have chosen it very carefully over all other breeds and all other

Before you leave the seller with your new Dalmatian puppy, make sure you have been given all of the proper documents that go with him.

The best way to help you pick the right Dalmatian puppy is to let the puppy have a say. The feeling of attraction should be mutual—pick the puppy that picks you!

When picking a new Dalmatian puppy, he should be outgoing and lively. If a puppy seems anxious or fearful, you may want to select another.

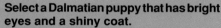

Select a Dalmatian puppy that has bright eyes and a shiny coat.

puppies. So before you ever get that Dalmatian puppy home, you will have prepared for its arrival by reading everything you can get your hands on having to do with the management of Dalmatians and puppies. True, you will run into many conflicting opinions, but at least you will not be starting "blind." Read, study, digest. Talk over your plans with your veterinarian, other "Dalmatian people," and the seller of your Dalmatian puppy.

When you get your Dalmatian puppy, you will find that your reading and study are far from finished. You've just scratched the surface in your plan to provide the greatest possible comfort and

Dalmatian puppies are fragile and must be handled with care. Because children are sometimes careless, observation when they are playing with puppies is a must!

When transporting your Dalmatian, whether a puppy or adult, a crate will protect the him and the car in case of car-sickness or other accidents.

health for your Dalmatian; and, by the same token, you do want to assure yourself of the greatest possible enjoyment of this wonderful creature. You must be ready for this puppy mentally as well as in the physical requirements.

TRANSPORTATION

If you take the puppy home by car, protect him from drafts, particularly in cold weather. Wrapped in a towel and carried in the arms or lap of a passenger, the Dalmatian puppy will usually make the trip without mishap. If the pup starts to drool and to squirm, stop the car for a few minutes. Have newspapers handy in case of car-sickness. A covered carton lined with newspapers provides protection for puppy and car, if you are driving alone. Avoid excitement and unnecessary handling of the puppy on arrival. A Dalmatian puppy is a very small "package" to be making a complete change of surroundings and company, and he needs frequent rest and refreshment to renew his vitality.

THE FIRST DAY AND NIGHT

When your Dalmatian puppy arrives in your home, put him down on the floor and don't pick him up again, except when it is absolutely necessary. He is a dog,

Never allow your Dalmatian to ride unrestricted. If an excited Dal gets under your feet it could cause an accident. Keep him in a car harness or crate when traveling. And never allow him to drive!

When you get your new Dalmatian puppy home handle him as little as possible. Let him get used to his new home and surroundings.

Although your Dalmatian puppy will take a little time to become comfortable in his new surroundings, he will soon fit right in.

a real dog, and must not be lugged around like a rag doll. Handle him as little as possible, and permit no one to pick him up and baby him. To repeat, *put your Dalmatian puppy on the floor or the ground and let him stay there except when it may be necessary to do otherwise.*

Quite possibly your Dalmatian puppy will be afraid for a while in his new surroundings, without his mother and littermates. Comfort him and reassure him, but don't console him. Don't give him the "oh-you-poor-itsy-bitsy-puppy" treatment. Be calm, friendly, and reassuring. Encourage him to walk around and sniff over his new home. If it's dark, put on the lights. Let him roam for a few minutes while you and everyone else concerned sit quietly or go about your routine business. Let the puppy come back to you.

Playmates may cause an immediate problem if the new Dalmatian puppy is to be greeted by children or other pets. If not, you can skip this subject. The natural affinity between puppies and children calls for some supervision until a live-and-let-live relationship is established. This applies particularly to a Christmas puppy, when there is more excitement than usual and more chance for a puppy to swallow something upsetting. It is a better plan to welcome the puppy several days before or after the holiday week. Like a baby, your Dalmatian puppy needs much rest and should not be over-handled. Once a child realizes that a puppy has "feelings" similar to his own, and can readily be hurt or injured, the opportunities for play and responsibilities provide exercise and training for both.

For his first night with you, he should be put where he is to sleep every night—say in the kitchen, since its floor can usually be easily cleaned. Let him explore the kitchen to his heart's content; close doors to confine him there. Prepare his food and feed him lightly the first night. Give him a pan with some water in it—not a lot, since most puppies will try to drink the whole pan dry. Give him an old coat or shirt to lie on. Since a coat or shirt will be strong in human scent, he will pick it out to

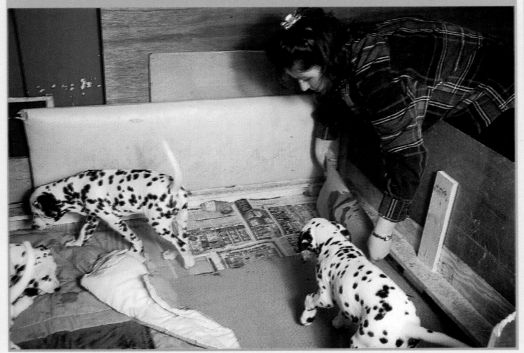

When housebreaking your Dal puppy, lay down a piece of paper that the dog has already urinated on over other papers so that he knows where he should go.

Bringing home a puppy or two or three could really make a wonderful difference in your life. Petting a dog is a proven way of relieving stress.

lie on, thus furthering his feeling of security in the room where he has just been fed.

HOUSEBREAKING HELPS

Now, sooner or later—mostly sooner—your new Dalmatian puppy is going to "puddle" on the floor. First take a newspaper and lay it on the puddle until the urine is soaked up onto the paper. *Save this paper.* Now take a cloth with soap and water, wipe up the floor and dry it well. Then take the wet paper and place it on a fairly large square of newspapers in a convenient corner. When cleaning up, always keep a piece of wet paper on top of the others. Every time he wants to "squat," he will seek out this spot and use the papers. (This routine is rarely necessary for more than three days.) Now leave your Dalmatian puppy for the night. Quite probably he will cry and howl a bit; some are more stubborn than others on this matter. But let him stay alone for the night. This may seem harsh treatment, but it is the best procedure in the long run. Just let him cry; he will weary of it sooner or later.

YOUR DALMATIAN'S HEALTH

As with many breeds, there are a few specific health problems common to the Dalmatian. Over the years, perhaps as a result of large scale breeding, the Dal's gene pool has become afflicted with a higher incidence of deafness than the normal canine random selection would dictate. Some Dal people claim there is a correlation between eye color and deafness, with the larger potential for deafness occurring with lighter-eyed dogs. Dals with liver-colored spots are likely to have lighter eyes. According to this theory, liver-spotted Dals are more likely to be born deaf. However, there is no scientific evidence to support this observation. There have been studies that refute this completely. Indeed, several leading breeders report breeding many generations of liver-spotted Dals without a single deaf pup. Black-spotted Dals almost always have dark eyes, although there are black Dals with blue or mixed color eyes.

Great progress has been made both in identifying deafness in pups and in genetic research. Dogs that are unilaterally deaf (deaf in one ear) and dogs that have a known history of deafness in their gene pool should be eliminated from all breeding programs. Only careful, selective, and responsible breeding by individuals whose devotion to the breed takes precedence over profit will eliminate this serious health problem endemic to the Dal. The Dal buyer can best protect himself by purchasing a dog only from a reputable breeder who has carefully

Keeping your Dalmatian healthy requires a good deal of attention and love. Knowing your dog's moods can help determine when he is sick—so get to know your dog!

and honestly recorded generational breedings and has used all necessary controls to keep deafness out of his programs.

Dalmatians are also prone to urinary problems, specifically urinary blockages caused by bladder stones. Among canines,

Exercise is a key factor in keeping your Dalmatian healthy. Dalmatians need regular exercise to maintain muscle tone and to keep from going "stir crazy."

the Dalmatian is unique in having a very high level of acid in its urine. This acid can crystallize and form stones, which can then cause blockages. While all Dalmatians carry the gene that causes this condition, only a percentage develop stones and blockages. To date, no effective way has been found to breed out the uric acid problem because the gene is so universal. The condition caused by the pressure of bladder stones can be very painful for the dog and sometimes requires surgery for relief.

Surgery should be avoided, if possible, and only used as a last resort if the crystals or stones cannot be expelled, dissolved, or passed in the urine. Hopefully the crystals can be flushed out before they form into stones in the bladder or urinary tract. There are two types of stones—one type can be broken down, and the other cannot. The type that can be broken down has been treated successfully in many cases with the drug, allopurinol. The other type of stone, once formed, can frequently be flushed out of the dog's system by inducing the dog to drink large amounts of water. This can sometimes be accomplished by adding salt to the dog's diet.

Prevention is always the best treatment. Breeders have had some success in reducing the incidence and severity of bladder stones by varying the Dalmatian's diet. Low protein diets in dog foods containing no more than 16-17% protein have been used along with very low protein canned specialty foods with less than 10% protein. Some breeders have used feeds that are essentially vegetable in composition. These dietary regimens have helped in many cases to sufficiently reduce the amount of uric acid to prevent the build-up of crystals.

While Dals have this genetic propensity and high levels of uric acid, some bloodlines have a greater incidence of stones than others. Buyers can learn something of the potential of a pup from the breeder. Stones are more likely to occur in dogs than in bitches. The problem is usually more easily treated in bitches. The most common age for the affliction to affect the dog is middle age. Dals that are household pets should be walked frequently at intervals no greater than three to four hours, especially for males. This helps to flush the urinary tract.

As with all dogs, the Dalmatian must receive yearly inoculations against rabies, distemper, leptospirosis, parvovirus, coronovirus. If you live in a wooded area, or exercise your Dal in the country, the dog should also be immunized for Lyme Disease. Needless to say, Dalmatian owners need to be observant and highly aware of the dog's unique urinary system and the special problems the pet may develop. Active conscientious coordination with your veterinarian will help overcome these problems. A careful and prudent owner will take pains to watch for signs of urinary problems by having their dogs checked frequently.

If you live in a wooded area, you will have fleas, ticks, and other parasites trying to latch onto your Dalmatian. Be sure to check him when he comes in from the outdoors.

Dalmatians with light colored eyes may have more problems with their hearing, although it is not scientifically proven.

Your Dalmatian should not be permitted to chew on anything from which he can bite sizable chunks. Gumabones® are made from strong polyurethane and are safe for dogs to chew on.

FEEDING YOUR DALMATIAN

Now let's talk about feeding your Dalmatian, a subject so simple that it's amazing there is so much nonsense and misunderstanding about it. Is it expensive to feed a Dalmatian? No, it is not! You can feed your Dalmatian economically and keep him in perfect shape the year round, or you can feed him expensively. He'll thrive either way, and let's see why this is true.

First of all, remember a Dalmatian is a dog. Dogs do not have a high degree of selectivity in their food, and unless you spoil them with great variety (and possibly turn them into poor, "picky" eaters) they will eat almost anything that they become accustomed to. Many dogs flatly refuse to eat nice, fresh beef. They pick around it and eat everything else. But meat—bah! Why? They aren't accustomed to it! They'd eat rabbit fast enough, but they refuse beef because they aren't used to it.

VARIETY NOT NECESSARY

A good general rule of thumb is forget all human preferences and don't give a thought to variety. Choose the right diet for your Dalmatian and feed it to him day after day, year after year, winter and summer. But what is the right diet?

Hundreds of thousands of dollars have been spent in canine nutrition research. The results are pretty conclusive, so you needn't go into a lot of experimenting with trials of this and that every other week. Research has proven just what your dog needs to eat and to keep healthy.

Dalmatians don't need a variety of foods to keep them happy and healthy. As a matter of fact, it will do just the opposite and make them picky eaters.

DOG FOOD

There are almost as many right diets as there are dog experts, but the basic diet most often recommended is one that consists of a dry food, either meal or kibble form. There are several of excellent quality, manufactured by reliable companies, research tested, and nationally advertised. They are inexpensive, highly satisfactory, and easily available in stores everywhere in containers of five to 50 pounds. Larger amounts cost less per pound, usually.

If you have a choice of brands, it is usually safer to choose the better known one; but even so, carefully read the analysis on the package. Do not choose any food in which the protein level is less than 25 percent, and be sure that this protein comes from both

Before and after meals, make sure your Dalmatian relaxes. Too much strenuous exercise could cause sickness.

Be sure to have fresh clean water available to your Dalmatian every day. An over-heated Dalmatian could present major problems.

animal and vegetable sources. The good dog foods have meat meal, fish meal, liver, and such, plus protein from alfalfa and soy beans, as well as some dried-milk product. Note the vitamin content carefully. See that they are all there in good proportions; and be especially certain that the food contains properly high levels of vitamins A and D, two of the most perishable and important ones. Note the B-complex level, but don't worry about carbohydrate and mineral levels. These substances are plentiful and cheap and not likely to be lacking in a good brand.

The advice given for how to choose a dry food also applies to moist or canned types of dog foods, if you decide to feed one of these.

Having chosen a really good food, feed it to your Dalmatian as the manufacturer directs. And once you've started, stick to it.

Never change if you can possibly help it. A switch from one meal or kibble-type food can usually be made without too much upset; however, a change will almost invariably give you (and your Dalmatian) some trouble.

WHEN SUPPLEMENTS ARE NEEDED

Now what about supplements of various kinds, mineral and vitamin, or the various oils? They added in concentrated form to the dog food you use. Except on the advice of your veterinarian, added amounts of vitamins can prove harmful to your Dalmatian! The same risk goes with minerals.

FEEDING SCHEDULE

When and how much food to give your Dalmatian? Most dogs do better if fed two or three

Dalmatians are notorious food burglars. If you allow them to eat from the table, they will soon learn to steal food when your back is turned.

are all okay to add to your Dalmatian's food. However, if you are feeding your Dalmatian a correct diet, and this is easy to do, no supplements are necessary unless your Dalmatian has been improperly fed, has been sick, or is having puppies. Vitamins and minerals are naturally present in all the foods; and to ensure against any loss through processing, they are smaller meals per day—this is not only better, but vital to larger and deep-chested dogs. As to how to prepare the food and how much to give, it is generally best to follow the directions on the food package. Your own Dalmatian may want a little more or a little less.

Fresh, cool water should always be available to your Dalmatian. This is important to good health

Nylafloss®, made with tough, long-lasting nylon string, is dental floss for your Dalmatian that removes plaque and tartar buildup. Unlike cotton tug toys, which are organic, Nylafloss® won't rot away.

throughout his lifetime.

ALL DALMATIANS NEED CHEWING

Puppies and young Dalmatians need something with resistance to chew on while their teeth and jaws are developing—for cutting the puppy teeth, to induce growth of the permanent teeth under the puppy teeth, to assist in getting rid of the puppy teeth at the proper time, to help the permanent teeth through the gums, to ensure normal jaw development, and to settle the permanent teeth solidly in the jaws.

The adult Dalmatian's desire to chew stems from the instinct for tooth cleaning, gum massage, and jaw exercise—plus the need for an outlet for periodic doggie tensions.

This is why dogs, especially puppies and young dogs, will often destroy property worth hundreds of dollars when their chewing instinct is not diverted from their owner's possessions. And this is why you should provide your Dalmatian with something to chew—something that has the necessary functional qualities, is desirable from the Dalmatian's viewpoint, and is safe for him.

It is very important that your Dalmatian not be permitted to chew on anything he can break or on any indigestible thing from which he can bite sizable chunks. Sharp pieces, such as from a bone which can be broken by a dog, may pierce the intestinal wall and kill. Indigestible things that can

The Gumabone® Frisbee®* is soft, safe and fun for all. The bone molded on the top allows Dalmatians to pick it up from flat surfaces without a problem. *The trademark Frisbee® is used under license from Mattel, Inc., California, USA.

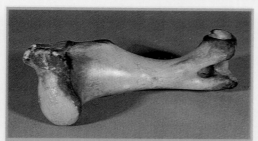

Pet shops sell real bones that have been colored, cooked, dyed or served natural. These are less safe than nylon bones.

be bitten off in chunks, such as from shoes or rubber or plastic toys, may cause an intestinal stoppage (if not regurgitated) and bring painful death, unless surgery is promptly performed.

Strong natural bones, such as 4- to 8-inch lengths of round shin bone from mature beef—either the kind you can get from a butcher or one of the variety available commercially in pet stores—may serve your Dalmatian's teething needs if his mouth is large enough to handle them effectively. You may be tempted to give your Dalmatian puppy a smaller bone and he may not be able to break it when you do, but puppies grow rapidly and the power of their jaws constantly increases until maturity. This means that a

All Nylabones® are strong—but no bone is as strong as the Galileo®, which is much stronger than the nylon from which it is created.

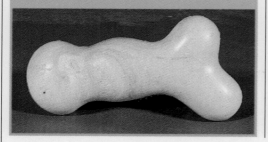

growing Dalmatian may break one of the smaller bones at any time, swallow the pieces, and die painfully before you realize what is wrong.

All hard natural bones are very abrasive. If your Dalmatian is an avid chewer, natural bones may wear away his teeth prematurely; hence, they then should be taken away from your dog when the teething purposes have been served. The badly worn, and usually painful, teeth of many mature dogs can be traced to

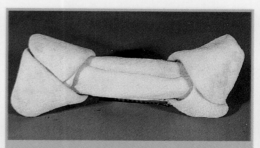

Rawhide is probably the best-selling dog chew. Traditional rawhide can be dangerous to dogs if unsupervised. Molded Roarhide® is safer and available in pet shops.

excessive chewing on natural bones.

Contrary to popular belief, knuckle bones that can be chewed up and swallowed by your Dalmatian provide little, if any, usable calcium or other nutriment. They do, however, disturb the digestion of most dogs and cause them to vomit the nourishing food they need.

Dried rawhide products of various types, shapes, sizes, and prices are available on the market and have become quite popular. However, they don't serve the primary chewing functions very

It is very important to keep your Dalmatian's teeth clean. You should examine your dog's mouth regularly.

the familiar dog shape. It is very hard and is eagerly accepted by Dalmatians. The melting process also sterilizes the rawhide. Don't confuse this with pressed rawhide, which is nothing more than small strips of rawhide squeezed together.

The nylon bones, especially those with natural meat and bone fractions added, are probably the most complete, safe, and economical answer to the chewing need. Dogs cannot break them or bite off sizable chunks; hence, they are completely safe—and being longer lasting than other things offered for the purpose, they are economical.

Hard chewing raises little

well; they are a bit messy when wet from mouthing, and most Dalmatians chew them up rather rapidly—but they have been considered safe for dogs until recently. Now, more and more incidents of death, and near death, by strangulation have been reported to be the results of partially swallowed chunks of rawhide swelling in the throat. More recently, some veterinarians have been attributing cases of acute constipation to large pieces of incompletely digested rawhide in the intestine.

A new product, molded rawhide, is very safe. During the process, the rawhide is melted and then injection molded into

Playtime is safest with a durable, soft Gumabone® Frisbee®*. It wouldn't be playtime without it! *The trademark Frisbee is used under license from Mattel, Inc., California, USA.

Nylabone® products, such as Hercules®, Nylaring® and Gumabone® are fun, safe chew toys that all Dalmatians can enjoy.

bristle-like projections on the surface of the nylon bones—to provide effective interim tooth cleaning and vigorous gum massage, much in the same way your toothbrush does it for you. The little projections are raked off and swallowed in the form of thin shavings, but the chemistry of the nylon is such that they break down in the stomach fluids and pass through without effect.

The toughness of the nylon provides the strong chewing resistance needed for important jaw exercise and effectively aids

A Gumabone® after chewing. The knobs develop elastic frays that act as a toothbrush.

Molded rawhide, called Roarhide® by Nylabone®, is very hard and safe for your dog. It is eagerly accepted by Dalmatians.

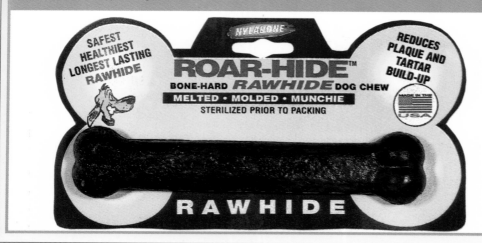

Because of their softer composition, Gumabones® are excellent chew toys for Dalmatian puppies. They come in a variety of shapes and sizes, and Dalmatians love to chew them.

teething functions, but there is no tooth wear because nylon is non-abrasive. Being inert, nylon does not support the growth of microorganisms; and it can be washed in soap and water or it can be sterilized by boiling or in an autoclave.

Nylabone® is highly recommended by veterinarians as a safe, healthy nylon bone that can't splinter or chip. Nylabone® is frizzled by the dog's chewing action, creating a toothbrush-like surface that cleanses the teeth and massages the gums. Nylabone®, the only chew products made of flavor-impregnated solid nylon, are available in your local pet shop. Nylabone® is superior to the cheaper bones because it is made of virgin nylon, which is the strongest and longest-lasting type of nylon available. The cheaper bones are made from recycled or re-ground nylon scraps, and have a tendency to break apart and split easily.

Nothing, however, substitutes for periodic professional attention for your Dalmatian's teeth and gums, not any more than your toothbrush can do that for you. Have your Dalmatian's teeth cleaned at least once a year by your veterinarian (twice a year is better) and he will be happier, healthier, and far more pleasant to live with.

Dalmatians can become very protective of their property. Never try to take away a dog's personal possession if you don't know the dog that well, especially a Nylabone® toy!

GROOMING THE DALMATIAN

The Dalmatian is a short-haired dog. The Dal sheds small white and hard to see black or liver-colored hairs. This is especially true during changes in season or temperature. Frequent bathing helps to control the shedding problem because it washes away the loose hair. Shedding can be even more of a problem for Dal owners than for owners of other shedding breeds. The Dal's hair is tough and has a small kink, or bend, at the end. This gives the hair the ability to cling tenaciously to furniture and clothes, and is quite difficult to remove as it doesn't brush off easily. Very fussy and fastidious people who crave order and neatness should not own Dalmatians.

Luckily, many Dal owners report that their dogs love baths and take naturally to soap and water. Dalmatian owners are cautioned that too much of a good thing is not good and that bathing more than once a week will dry out the dog's skin and is counterproductive.

Happily, the Dal's short white coat helps owners with tick and flea problems because the coat makes it a less receptive host for these parasites than longer haired breeds. Again, bathing and some grooming vigilance along with a sensible use of anti-pest devices and programs, will help control the

Frequent bathing helps to keep shedding to a minimum. As much as Dalmatians love a good bath, don't over do it because too much bathing can dry out your dog's skin.

Those Dals with sensitive skin problems such as scaling and dryness may need special food formulas like lamb and rice to ensure healthy skin and coat. The Dal should be brushed occasionally, preferably in an open space, to remove any dead hair that has not been bathed away. This is particularly true in warmer weather.

The Dalmatian is principally a white dog, and as with most white pets, it will show any dirt more dramatically than a colored breed. For this reason, the Dal should always be kept clean and neat. Many owners clip their dog's whiskers. Any areas where the dog's hair stands out and prevents the appearance of a smooth outline can be clipped. This is usually done on the lower legs and paw areas. The toenails should also be cut at regular intervals.

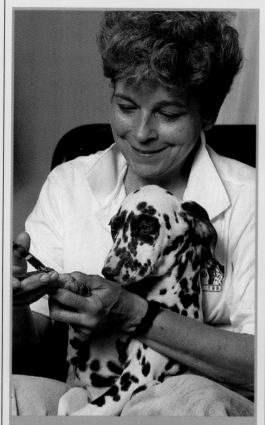

Begin clipping your Dalmatian's nails at an early age so that he becomes used to it. Nails should be clipped regularly.

Many owners cut their Dalmatian's whiskers to help give the appearance of a dog that is neat and well groomed.

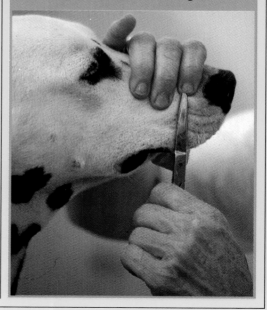

potential threat of parasites to the dog's general health. Dals can develop skin allergies associated with dry skin, but this is not a special problem in the breed.

Color and markings are extremely important characteristics in the Dalmatian. For show purposes, the better distributed and more defined the spots, the better the dog. Coat maintenance is of paramount importance. The hair of a Dal is not only short but should also be hard, dense, and shiny. Good, sound nutrition goes a long way to insure that the Dal's coat will achieve its full potential.

TRAINING YOUR DALMATIAN

You owe proper training to your Dalmatian. The right and privilege of being trained is his birthright; and whether your Dalmatian is going to be a handsome, well-mannered housedog and companion, a show dog, or whatever possible use he may be put to, the basic training is always the same—all must start with basic obedience, or what might be called "manner training."

Your Dalmatian must come instantly when called and obey the "Sit" or "Down" command just as fast; he must walk quietly at "Heel," whether on or off lead. He must be mannerly and polite wherever he goes; he must be polite to strangers on the street and in stores. He must be mannerly in the presence of other dogs. He must not bark at children on roller skates, motorcycles, or other domestic animals. And he must be restrained from chasing cats. It is not a dog's inalienable right to chase cats, and he must be reprimanded for it.

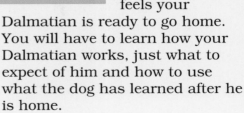

A well-trained Dalmatian will wait by the door when he needs to go out.

PROFESSIONAL TRAINING

How do you go about this training? Well, it's a very simple procedure, pretty well standardized by now. First, if you can afford the extra expense, you may send your Dalmatian to a professional trainer, where in 30 to 60 days he will learn how to be a "good dog." If you enlist the services of a good professional trainer, follow his advice of when to come to see the dog. No, he won't forget you, but too-frequent visits at the wrong time may slow down his training progress. And using a "pro" trainer means that you will have to go for some training, too, after the trainer feels your Dalmatian is ready to go home. You will have to learn how your Dalmatian works, just what to expect of him and how to use what the dog has learned after he is home.

OBEDIENCE TRAINING CLASS

Another way to train your Dalmatian (many experienced Dalmatian people think this is the best) is to join an obedience

Your Dalmatian must come instantly when you call him. This is part of the "manner training" that every dog must have.

The best gift is a healthy, happy and lovable puppy. The Dalmatian, if properly trained and cared for, will grow into an outstanding family member and true companion.

training class right in your own community. There is such a group in nearly every community nowadays. Here you will be working with a group of people who are also just starting out. You will actually be training your own dog, since all work is done under the direction of a head trainer who will make suggestions

As in human behavior, puppies will often imitate their parents behavior. A well- trained adult Dalmatian can be a wonderful help in training puppies.

And, what is more important, he will learn to do exactly what he is told to do, no matter how much

When your Dalmatian does what you command, reward him with a gentle pat and vocal praise—that is is all he needs.

Your Dalmatian must learn to stay by your side, whether on or off lead.

to you and also tell you when and how to correct your Dalmatian's errors. Then, too, working with such a group, your Dalmatian will learn to get along with other dogs.

confusion there is around him or how great the temptation is to go his own way.

Write to your national kennel club for the location of a training club or class in your locality. Sign up. Go to it regularly—every session! Go early and leave late! Both you and your Dalmatian will benefit tremendously.

TRAIN HIM BY THE BOOK

The third way of training your Dalmatian is by the book. Yes, you can do it this way and do a good job of it too. But in using the book method, select a book, buy it, study it carefully; then study it some more, until the procedures are almost second nature to you. Then start your training. But stay with the book and its advice and exercises.

Successful Dog Training is one of the better dog training books by Hollywood dog trainer Michael Kamer, who trains dogs for movie stars.

If your Dalmatian won't obey you even after you've trained him or you're not making any progress during training, it may be best to go to a professional trainer or an obedience training class.

Don't start in and then make up a few rules of your own. If you don't follow the book, you'll get into jams you can't get out of by yourself. If after a few hours of short training sessions your Dalmatian is still not working as he should, get back to the book for a study session, because it's your fault, not the dog's! The procedures of dog training have been so well systemized that it must be your fault, since literally thousands of fine Dalmatians have been trained by the book.

After your Dalmatian is "letter perfect" under all conditions, then, if you wish, go on to advanced training and trick work.

Your Dalmatian will love his obedience training, and you'll burst with pride at the finished product! Your Dalmatian will enjoy life even more, and you'll enjoy your Dalmatian more. And remember—you *owe good training to your Dalmatian.*

When your Dal has mastered basic obedience, you can move on to other types of training. Jerry, owned by Elizabeth Davies, shows off his fetching abilities.

Dalmatians can also be taught to wear protective or fashionable "doggie" clothing. Things such as raincoats and safety harnesses can come in handy in times of need.

SHOWING YOUR DALMATIAN

A show Dalmatian is a comparatively rare thing. He is one out of several litters of puppies. He happens to be born with a degree of physical perfection that closely approximates the standard by which the breed is judged in the show ring. Such a dog should, on maturity, be able to win or approach his championship in good, fast company at the larger shows. Upon finishing his championship, he is apt to be as highly desirable as a breeding animal. As a proven stud, he will automatically command a high price for service.

Showing Dalmatians is a lot of fun—yes, but it is a highly competitive sport. While all the experts were once beginners, the odds are against a novice. You will be showing against experienced handlers, often people who have devoted a lifetime to breeding, picking the right ones, and then showing those dogs through to their championships. Moreover, the most perfect Dalmatian ever born has faults, and in your hands the faults will be far more evident than with the experienced

handler who knows how to minimize his Dalmatian's faults. These are but a few points on the sad side of the picture.

The experienced handler, as I say, was not born knowing the ropes. He learned—*and so can you!* You can if you will put in the same time, study and keen observation that he did. But it will take time!

Finding a show champion Dalmatian is a rare thing. Such a dog is highly prized for breeding purposes.

KEY TO SUCCESS

First, search for a truly fine show prospect. Take the puppy home, raise him by the book, and as carefully as you know how, give him every chance to mature into the Dalmatian you hoped for. My advice is to keep your dog out of big shows, even Puppy Classes, until he is mature. Maturity in the male is roughly two years; with the female, 14 months or so. When your Dalmatian is approaching maturity, start out at match shows, and, with this experience for both of you, then go gunning for the big wins at the big shows.

Next step, read the standard by which the Dalmatian is judged. Study it until you know it by heart. Having done this, and while your puppy is at home (where he should be) growing into a normal, healthy Dalmatian, go to every dog show you can possibly reach. Sit at the ringside and watch Dalmatian judging. Keep your ears and eyes open. Do your own judging, holding each of those dogs against the standard, which you now know by heart.

In your evaluations, don't start looking for faults. Look for the virtues—the best qualities. How does a given Dalmatian shape up against the standard? Having looked for and noted the virtues, then note the faults and see what prevents a given Dalmatian from standing correctly or moving well. Weigh these faults against the virtues, since, ideally, every feature of the dog should contribute to the harmonious whole dog.

"RINGSIDE JUDGING"

It's a good practice to make notes on each Dalmatian, always holding the dog against the standard. In "ringside judging," forget your personal preference for this or that feature. What does the standard say about it? Watch carefully as the judge places the dogs in a given class. It is difficult from the ringside always to see why number one was placed over the second dog. Try to follow the judge's reasoning. Later try to talk with the judge after he is finished. Ask him questions as to why he placed certain Dalmatians and not others. Listen while the judge explains his placings, and, I'll say right here, any judge worthy of his license should be able to give reasons.

When you're not at the ringside, talk with the fanciers and breeders who have Dalmatians.

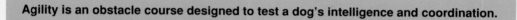
Agility is an obstacle course designed to test a dog's intelligence and coordination.

Don't be afraid to ask opinions or say that you don't know. You have a lot of listening to do, and it will help you a great deal and speed up your personal progress if you are a good listener.

THE NATIONAL CLUB

You will find it worthwhile to join the national Dalmatian club and to subscribe to its magazine. From the national club, you will learn the location of an approved regional club near you. Now, when your young Dalmatian is eight to ten months old, find out the dates of match shows in your section of the country. These differ from regular shows only in that no championship points are given. These shows are especially designed to launch young dogs (and new handlers) on a show career.

ENTER MATCH SHOWS

With the ring deportment you have watched at big shows firmly in mind and practice, enter your Dalmatian in as many match shows as you can. When in the ring, you have two jobs. One is to see to it that your Dalmatian is always being seen to its best advantage. The other job is to keep your eye on the judge to see what he may want you to do next. Watch only the judge and your Dalmatian. Be quick and be alert; do exactly as the judge directs. Don't speak to him except to answer his questions. If he does something you don't like, don't say so. And don't irritate the judge (and everybody else) by constantly talking and fussing with your dog.

In moving about the ring, remember to keep clear of dogs beside you or in front of you. It is my advice to you *not* to show your Dalmatian in a regular point show until he is at least close to maturity and after both you and your dog have had time to perfect ring manners and poise in the match shows.

Dalmatian clearing the bar jump at an agility trial. Agility can be fun for both dog and owner.